Gratitude
is my
Superpower

Alicia Ortego

This Superpower
belongs to

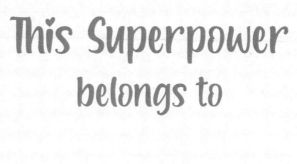

· ·

· ·

Every day, I am grateful for so many things;
for the sun that warms and the bird that sings.
I am grateful for my family and friends,
for the books I write, and for my pens.

I am grateful for the raindrops and the beautiful rainbow,
for the trees and flowers, and for the first snow.
I am grateful to my little readers and their parents too.
That's why I dedicated this book to YOU.

Hi my name is Betsy and this is **Mr. T**
I am only 7 but he is **70!**

You wouldn't know to look at him, he never seems to **age,**
He slowly moves around the house and doesn't have a **cage.**

One day when I was playing with him, I suddenly felt quite **sad,**
"What's the matter?" Mum said, "You're usually so **glad."**

"It's Mr. T," I said to her,
"I think there's something **wrong.**

To carry that big house all day,
he has to be so **strong.**

"Do you think it stops him,
from having fun like **me?**

I've never seen him run or jump
as happy as can **be."**

"Oh my dear you mustn't worry, Mr. T is **fine**.
Turtles have different needs in life,
they're not like yours or **mine**.

"The nature of a turtle is harmless, quiet and **shy,**
They love to hide inside their shells when people pass them **by.**

So Mr. T is very grateful for everything he's **got,**
Which means he doesn't worry, about things he has **not.**

"Let's play a game together," Mum said,
"I call it **Gratitude,**
It'll help you understand Mr. T,
are you in the **mood?"**

Mum takes me to the garden and just behind the **flowers**
Picking up a stone she says, "This has **SUPERPOWERS!**

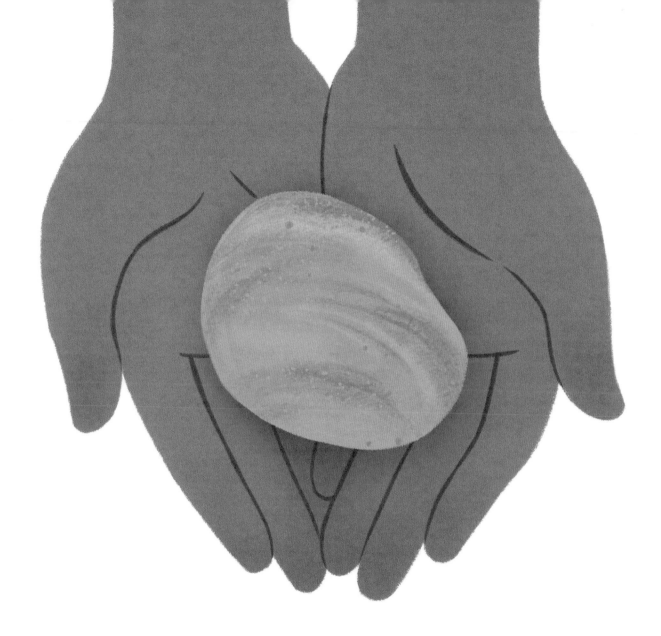

"Every time you're upset when things don't go as **planned,**
You take out your Gratitude stone and hold it in your **hand.**
The stone will work its magic and soon you'll begin to **see,**
Everything that's happening is how it's meant to **be.**"

No sooner had we gone inside,
the sky began to **rain,**
Tears began to fill my eyes,
I wanted to go out **again!**

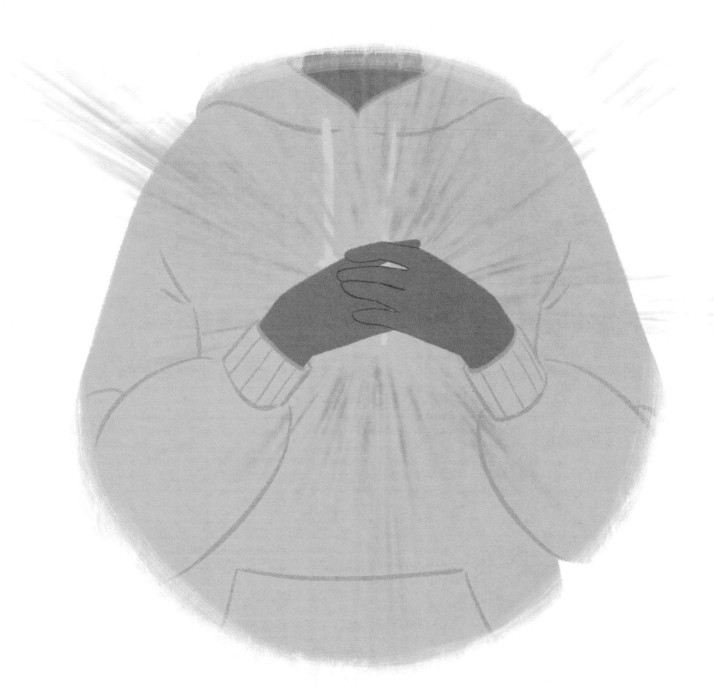

Remembering my special stone, I squeezed with all my **might,**
What could I be grateful for when rain was in my **sight?**

But just then I remembered, without it, plants won't **grow,**
Fish wouldn't live in the sea and rivers wouldn't **flow.**

"Thank you sky for raining, you're really rather **clever,**
Now I know the job you do, you can rain **whenever.**"

Next morning when it's time to wake,
my body's filled with **dread,**
Going to school is the last thing I want,
I'd rather stay home **instead!**

Beneath my pillow is my stone, I squeeze it once **again,**
Remembering the friends I'd see and my teacher, **Mrs. Blaine.**

At school I had forgotten, today was **Sibling Day.**
I don't have any siblings so I didn't know what to **say.**

My stone will have the answer, I thought, I'll squeeze it and we'll **see.**
"Of course," I said, "I am grateful, because I have **Mr. T!**"

At dinner time it worked again
when mum put down my **plate,**
No yummy cake but rice and veg,
which I didn't **appreciate!**

But then I remembered the children
who aren't as lucky as **me,**
To have a healthy, warm meal,
cooked by their **mummy.**

At bedtime when I'm not tired and want to play **instead**,
I'm grateful for my turtle pjs and warm and cozy **bed.**

But just then I remember,
I'm not even carrying the **stone,**
"Mum," I shout, "I did Gratitude
and I did it on my **own!"**

"Of course you did, my darling,
because Gratitude is in **there.**"
Upon my heart she places her hand,
with the other she strokes my **hair.**

"So Gratitude's in all of us," I said,
"And all we have to **do,**
Is stop and think how thankful we are
instead of feeling **blue!"**

Next day during playtime, there is a new boy **there,**
With shiny braces on his teeth and curly, light brown **hair.**

Tears are falling down his face, he wished he had not **moved,**
A decision made by his parents and he had not **approved!**

I tell him of the Gratitude stone and ask if we can **find,**
Something to be thankful for that he can bear in **mind.**

He holds the stone and thinks a minute, a smile across his **face,**
"I'm thankful for our new home, the garden has so much **space!"**

Now every time I go out
I make sure to have with **me,**
At least one stone to pass on,
along with my **story.**

The more we share about Gratitude
the happier we will **be,**
Will you share this story
and help other children like **me?**

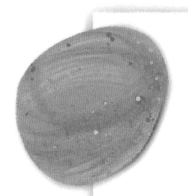

5 Days Gratitude Journal
for Kids

Find a nice stone and carry it for 5 days with you
to remind you to be thankful.
In the evening write 3 things
you could be thankful for during this day.

I am thankful for

This person

This thing

This place

This food

This hobby

Dear reader,

Thank you for trusting us and reading our book. We would appreciate it if you would let us know your impressions. Please take two minutes and share your thoughts and observations with the millions who are waiting for your feedback.

Alicia Ortego

BOOKS FOR KIDS

From the author:

This book is written for all children to help them feel the magic of gratitude. Although they often crave more, our job is to teach our little ones to be grateful for what they have.

"Gratitude is my superpower" teaches children that happiness is in everyday things, both small and big ones. With the help of this book, children will begin to appreciate their parents and friends, but they will also get to know their emotions.

This story will bring a smile back to the little ones' faces when they realize that everything they need is already at their fingertips.

'Gratitude is my Superpower' is the fourth book in 'My Superpower Series' - the growth mindset books for kids, suitable for all ages and we hope it will be enjoyed by all parents, grandparents, teachers and independent school readers.

Visit my website for more information and free printables. www.aliciaortego.com or scan the code below

Thank you again for your support!

— Alicia Ortego

Collect them all!

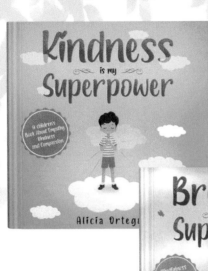

Kindness is my **Superpower**

A Children's Book About Empathy, Kindness and Compassion

Alicia Ortego

Breathing is my **Superpower**

Mindfulness Book for Kids to Feel Calm and Peaceful

Alicia Ortego

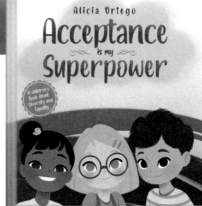

Alicia Ortego

Acceptance is my **Superpower**

A Children's Book About Diversity and Equality